HUGH MCMILLAN is a poet from Penpont in Dumfries and Galloway. He has written five full collections of poetry and has read in events and poetry festivals worldwide. His pamphlet *Postcards from the Hedge* was a winner of the Callum Macdonald Prize in 2009, a prize he won again for *Sheepenned* in 2017; as part of that prize, he became Michael Marks Poet in Residence for the Harvard Summer School in Napflio, Greece. He was also a winner of the Smith Doorstep Poetry Prize and the Cardiff International Poetry Competition. *Devorgilla's Bridge* was shortlisted for the Michael Marks Award and in 2015 was shortlisted for the Basil Bunting Poetry Award. In 2014 Hugh was awarded the first literature commission by the Wigtown Book Festival to create a work inspired by John Mactaggart's *The Scottish Gallovidian Encyclopaedia* (1824); *McMillan's Galloway* was published in limited edition in 2014 and in a revised edition from Luath in 2015.

By the same author:

Tramontana, Dog and Bone, 1990
Horridge, Chapman, 1995
Aphrodite's Anorak, Peterloo Poets, 1996
Strange Bamboo, Shoestring, 2007
Postcards from the Hedge, Roncadora Press, 2009
Devorgilla's Bridge, Roncadora Press, 2010
Cairn, Roncadora Press, 2011
Thin Slice of Moon, Roncadora Press, 2012
McMillan's Galloway, privately printed, 2015
Not Actually being in Dumfries, Luath Press, 2015
McMillan's Galloway: A Creative Guide by an Unreliable Local, Luath Press, 2017
Sheepenned, Roncadora Press, 2017

Heliopolis

HUGH McMILLAN

Luath Press Limited
EDINBURGH
www.luath.co.uk

First published 2018

ISBN: 978-1-912147-76-2

The author's right to be identified as author of this book
under the Copyright, Designs and Patents Act 1988 has been asserted.

The paper used in this book is recyclable. It is made
from low chlorine pulps produced in a low energy, low emission
manner from renewable forests.

Printed and bound by Bell & Bain Ltd., Glasgow.

Typeset in 11 point Sabon

© Hugh McMillan 2018

Contents

Acknowledgements   9
Introduction   11

Section One: Daemons

Crazy Dancer   16
Ghost Dancing in the Gallowgate 1892   18
The Beating   19
Carsethorn   21
Descent   22
Cottage   24
Pier Head   25
James McMichael   26
The Sunken Garden of Eliza Stott   27
Vatersay 1853/ Kos 2015   28
Summerisle   29
The Old Fort at Grennan   30
Accounting for Elspeth McQueen, Kirkcudbright 1689   31
Durham Excavation Skeleton 22   32
Dumfries Schoolgirls, 1960s   33
Christmas is Coming   34
Sunday in Oban   35
Gordon Johnstone Remembers   36
Red Letter Day   38
Spiral   39
Lost Boy   40
Bells   41
Fishy   42
Coming out for Caleb   43

The Magic Hours	44
The Psychic Detective Jim Gilpin	46
The Archive	47

Section Two: Hyporborea

Asini/Calinish	50
Grave Goods	51
Parga	52
Littoral	53
On the Caul	54
Epistle to Robert Burns	56
Paddy Kelly and the Banjo Tree	57
Queran's Well	58
Bus station in the wind	59
Watcher	60
Crarie Knowe	61
Et in Arcadia Ego	62
When the Wifi's Down	63
Drowned	64
The Conversion of Sheep	65
Let's Hear it for the Homo Naledi	66
Nihilists	67
The Shades of One Shade	68
The Lemon Enclosure	69

Section Three: Ekphrasis

Bacchus and Ariadne	72
Circe and the Crème de Menthe	73
Diana and Acteon	74
Hylas is Surprised by Seven Nymphs in a Lily Pond	75

Helen of Troy	76
Perspehone	77
Poetry Doubles, Lesbos	78

Section Four: Latro

Lest We Forget	80
364 BC	82
Jubilation	83
Dania Ersheid, on her way home from school	85
Overheard in the Buccleuch and Queensberry Hotel	87
Green	88
The Salon, Buccleuch Hotel	90
Peace in Our Time	91
Markers	92
Silk with a White Eagle	93
Reflections on Heritage in a Galloway Harbour	95
Mongrels	97
Rummaging in a Box on St Andrew's Day	99
Scotland's Hidden Gems	101
September 2014	102

Section Five: Oikia

Birthday	104
A Proper Joke	106
Psalm 121	108
Castle Building	109
Last Post	111
Late	112
Bryony Patterson and the Poetry Machine	113
My Birthday	115
Janice	116

Road Trip	118
Rosemary is Remembering	119
Reading *Electric Brae* Before the Plane	120
The Airwaves	121
The Nymphaeum	122
Where the Burn Joins the River	123
The Christmas Box	124

Section Six: Foteinos

Tuesday Night Ciutadella	128
Poetry	129
Hope	130
Nativity	131
Nunc Scio Quid Sit Amor	133
That Time of Night	134
Lit	135

Acknowledgements

Some of these poems have appeared previously in *New Writing Scotland*, *Gutter*, *The Dark Horse*, *Northwords*, *The Glasgow Review*, *Cordite*, *Taheke*, *Verity La*, the *Australian Poetry Journal*, *The Rialto*, *The Poetry Review*, the *Scotsman*, the *Antigonish Review* and in the pamphlet *Sheepenned* (Roncadora Press 2017).

Introduction
Second Beauty

Hugh McMillan is a former history teacher with a special interest in the Byzantine period. Consequently, Hugh would have revelled in his residency at the Harvard School of Hellenic Studies in Nafpilo, Greece in the summer of 2017 – the reward of winning the Callum Macdonald Memorial Award for the pamphlet *Sheepenned*. I was one of the judges for the prize. I was struck by both the lyrical beauty and aesthetic ambition of the work.

In his preface to *The Lemon Tree* by Margaret Ruddock, William Butler Yeats wrote 'works of lyric genius, when the circumstances of their origin is known, gain a second beauty, passing as it were out of literature and becoming life'. Equally adept in writing in the lyrical and modern, McMillan, like Yeats, often sails into the mystic – the place of the magic hours: 'Now the sick summer's gone/ with its smoke and mirrors/ we can come into our own; all the shades of one shade;' ('The Shades of One Shade'). In Classical Greece a shade or σκιά literally meant the ghost of the dead. In McMillan's world, winter in Dumfries and Galloway – the resting place of Robert Burns – becomes the season of ghosts.

There are numerous references to Hellenic culture and mythology throughout the sections of this book: Daemons conjures the spectres of things and people past; Hyperboea, a meditation on other places and times; Ekiphrasis, work inspired by visual art; Latro, a series of vexations; Oikia, reflections on family and kinship; and Foteinos, strange moments of enlightenment.

There are parallels between McMillan's Dumfries and Galloway and the fabled Byzantium recounted by Yeats. The artisan perfection of Classical Greece in Yeats' eyes is everlasting, potent and watchful:

> Once out of nature I shall never take
> My bodily form from any natural thing,
> But such a form as Grecian goldsmiths make
> Of hammered gold and gold enamelling
> To keep a drowsy Emperor awake;
>
> Or set upon a golden bough to sing
> To lords and ladies of Byzantium
> Of what is past, or passing, or to come.
> ('Sailing to Byzantium', WB Yeats)

Through the lens of McMillan, the discovery of a Byzantine artefact in Dumfries and Galloway induces a dream-state, a ghostly reminder. The emperor, once woke, is now entombed:

> When I heard Byzantine silk
> Had turned up here
>
> It was like saying someone
> Had uncovered a pot of dreams,
> the meeting of impossible worlds
> made possible by men
>
> who lived here long before us, before the Emperor
> himself was tombed in legend.
> ('Silk with a White Eagle', Hugh McMillan)

Yeats upheld the Greek notion that a great poet is inspired and possessed by the Muses, daughters of all powerful Zeus and Mnemosyne, goddess of memory. The Muses represented epic poetry, history, song, love, tragedy, hymn, dance, comedy and astronomy. Each are interwoven in sections of this book. Of all the Muses, it was surprising to find few expressions of love (erotic or amorous). The most explicit reference being: 'Someone's night is always alive/ with sentences/ rhythmic and sleepless as cicadas/ punctuated now and ever, with love.' ('The Airwaves'). Whereas Yeats had a quest for 'life at its intense moments', McMillan commonly reverts to bathos for subverting the sublime and the pompous in equal measure. His playful affection is reserved for the Muses of history and, most rewardingly, comedy: 'can't imagine what'll be like/ when you finally undress,/ the walls will come down.' ('Helen of Troy').

The poems in this collection are the hammered gold and enamelling of a master craftsman. They effortlessly pass out of literature and become life. In his 'Epistle to Robert Burns (during a Depression in the North Atlantic)' the poet writes that 'the human experiment has failed in mid Nithsdale.' This statement acquires a contradictory second beauty as we know this statement cannot ring true with a writer of McMillan's abilities in locus.

Asif Khan
Director
Scottish Poetry Library

Section One

Daemons

Crazy Dancer

After a session in the Saracen's Head
Crazy Dancer was arrested for affray
and got a month in gaol.
The magistrate was not aware

of the Indian Wars
but had seen enough drunken Scots
to last a lifetime:
the sentence was short.

It was a long way from Crooked Fall
to Barlinnie, via a train
of towns too mired in rain
and miserable to recall

but each day he'd worked,
been fed,
though at night he saw
the river leaking blood,

heard the shrill screams
of children, high and ebbing
still like birds,
dreams or waking.

He played his death for crowds
of faces round as moons
and it was true, the Nanissanah,
what the preacher crooned

in the last clasp of summer
when the stars were still there:
he couldn't die;
he would remember.

Ghost Dancing in the Gallowgate 1892

After one whisky too many
Crazy Dancer
thumped a minder
over the head with a doorstop

but before that had reached
an understanding
beyond the need for words
with Donald from Sligachan

whose leg was shot off
in Egypt with the Seaforths.
They both lived in
the hem of their histories

ragged at the edges
telling stories for beer
over and over
in the insistent poetry of tongues

as though the fevered act
of repetition might
reel back time
and the landscapes
black with ghosts.

The Beating

There's a grainy photograph:
two Sioux laying a wreath
at Burns' grave 1904.
The beaten honouring the beaten.

Where today are the Pequot?
the Narragansett,
the Mohican,
the Pokanoket?

They are bought and sold
for English gold,
melted as snow
before the summer sun.

Poetry and death
is how legends are made.
There is a story
we have Indian blood

my daughters and I:
some quirk of genealogy,
the diaspora,
the Gàidhealtachd,
the cold plains of Canada.

I know it's true
when I hear the high ghosts
of geese,
when my breath freezes,
when that last note of a song

lingers long, like pain.
When I hear our
rivers of blood
beating to the sea.

Carsethorn

The flowers of the Solway
are garden high,
driftwood, wrack and plastic,
but the sea has gone.
In Carsethorn now
it's Sunday roast
in a pub panelled
and kitsched like a poop-deck.
We will chew and bray
and maybe squeeze
the sticky toffee pudding in,
and watch the grey kidney
of mud that stretches to
Annan and Silloth,
beyond to Richibucto
the Baie de Chalou,
down the silt slash to limbo,
21,000 in a single year
from a single pier,
now black bones.
The Lovely Nell took 82
the only reason written in the log
'for bread'.

Descent

Those tight bunned women
and fierce men are framed
always against a grey sky,
frozen on film like DNA.
Dogs lolling at their feet,

they are by their cottages,
at the doorstep or on benches
with a trellis of honeysuckle
behind. Only occasionally
is there a hint of hill or sea,
mostly they are framed by wall,

the same wall that their parents
posed by in photographs that grew
dark then disappeared.
Their children decamped
to other cottages nearby,
you see them in censuses

and birth certificates:
they were seamstresses,
fishermen, light keepers,
all rooted in the soil and mortar
until in a sunburst
they were scattered by war

or joblessness,
taken by their necks
and rained all over the world.

Altcreich, Traigh Mhor, Fonn Aline
have paved patio areas now.
500 pounds a week, no pets

but the views are to die for.

Cottage

In steady rain
the walls rear up,
every other sign
gone to moss,

no garden,
no patch of kail,
only this, broken
on a hillside,

a space
where rituals
of birth and death
and work

were acted out,
almost in cloud.
Lit by candlelight
the faces here

for fifty years,
now in bloodlines,
or dreams.
The roof came in,

then cold stars.

Pier Head

Two burning bars of mud
going gold to where the river
opens up like a mouth.

Arrows they say:
follow the geese past the skirts
of the mountain

and out to the sea that seems limp
but laps at every land.
Here on the shore we build everything

in imitation of it,
our benches like skiffs,
our houses like upturned shells.

In the sun we shine,
salt on our skin.
See the old ones waddle –

seals at twilight, they are estuary men,
barking wanly into the night.
The young, these few,

let us look jealously at them though,
with their iphones and nonchalance,
packed ready to go.

James McMichael

Fallow Wheat our farm was called
and we were harvested
one by one:
Esther two months six days,
Henrietta eight years,
lovely Jessie twelve,
their mother at thirty nine.
These beautiful sick hills!
The minister says the righteous
have a place at God's side:
for the rest of us there's Illinois.

The Sunken Garden of Eliza Stott

I imagine it, the fire of bloom,
the buds, espaliers,
their calligraphy pointing to

the peach house.
I hear water on rocks,
the black pool that never brims.

He complained.
No view of the river,
the slip of the sea that made

his fortune, delivered up his wife.
She only wanted the sky,
the trees lattice,

the sound of birds
in dead leaves.
Such echoes she heard!

When he died –
it was the age for dying young –
she left in one night.

Now there's nothing:
a boundary wall, a bench,
a public toilet with a reputation,

and even if you climb,
strain the eyes, still no view
of the way to Philadelphia

Vatersay 1853/ Kos 2015

The boats go out,
come back with their catch,
bundles, boxes, bodies,
returned to the barren lands
and buried in a pit.
When autumn gales lash
a beach thin as a smile
we find children lying
in the shallows,
kissing the sea.

Summerisle

'Dog shite and plenty af it.'
Big Tem is talking of his cucumbers,
great phalluses,
thick and rubbered enough
to crack your head.
'The carrots dinnae like it,
they prefer human keech.'

What luck to be born here
in this verdant space,
though our cottages slip into the sea
and we are a place
for ghosts and shotguns
and fine views of the cosmos
uncluttered by street light

because our streets are empty,
only the regeneration offices open,
winking long into the diamond night.
In Spring the auld heids
will stamp around the maypole,
their caps cocked at the breeze
and we will count the missing:

our children gone
over the hills like fairies,
their replacements grim changelings
with water for blood
the Daily Telegraph for a newspaper,
and not enough shite for a carrot,
if they tried all year.

The Old Fort at Grennan

Miles, and nothing alive
though an oystercatcher
calls somewhere, sadly.
Dykes twist to the horizon.
Where are the men who built them?
Gone to Nova Scotia
with their pipes and neckerchiefs.
On either side of the walls,
new wire restrains livestock
that's not there either,
to show that someone, somewhere,
owns this land, has a grant to prove it.
I climb, emerge onto the crest,
and a hare bounds off into cloud.
On top, with its boulders and sheep skulls,
its faint scars of ditch,
with a hollow wind through the thorns,
Grennan nails empty land to empty sky.

Accounting for Elspeth McQueen, Kirkcudbright 1689

3 pounds for peat
16 shillings for coal
4 for rope, 4 for a tar barrel
8 for a drum beat.

The stink came free.
The smoke curled
in clouds above the Tolbooth,
cut off the light all day.

The minister
said his horse sweated blood
when they brought her in,
that she spoiled

her neighbours milk.
Guid folk all,
few there that day
beyond the executioner

who cost the council,
they noted, a pint at the start,
seven more
while she burned.

Durham Excavations
Skeleton 22

Galloway wis bauch-hertit fir the King
but hunger an adventur
are gowsterous sairjants,
an oor dreich hills
grow sojers like teeth.

We foucht fur the Covenant
an agin England
an, taen, wur mairched
sooth, frae graff
tae sorry graff.

Mony were shot fur sport,
mony selt fur slaves, sent
on boats ower the undevaulin seas.
The lave?
The rats haed us.

Dumfries Schoolgirls, 1960s

Girls are making their way
past the pointillism
of flowers, the backdrop
of Greyfriars lit
like honey.

School is out. In mid lunge,
arm in arm, their books clasped,
they are moving off picture
as fast as this moment
will allow.

Bless this photographer,
historian, voyeur, pervert,
bless him in his cold cell,
his eyrie, his cramped room,
he has brought them back

from the noose of years,
from children, worry, disease,
death, brought them back
to walk briskly here always,
bathed in light.

Christmas is Coming

Christmas is coming.
Miles of wet dyke
and twisted trees,
the ribs of cottages.
The day is broken,
splintered at our feet.

In the street,
a woman asks me to read
a message on her phone,
her eyes are bad.
It is from Violet, it says
where are you?
Violet is dead she explains,
this is now the only way
we communicate.

Christmas is coming.
In the mist,
dots of light prism,
lead somewhere.

Sunday in Oban

How quickly the Oban
of the glass sea,
of the lines of islands
shaking in
mist like bright steam,
of the warm pubs
and fairy lights,

how quickly that Oban
becomes the Oban
of the cement sky,
the drowned chip paper,
the little boats
shivered by waves,
the cold coffee
and smudged windowpane.

How quickly the Oban
of getting there
becomes the Oban of
needing to go,
the Oban you've imagined,
seen even,
in the long dreamy
footlights of your memory
becomes the Oban
dissolving now
in quite ordinary rain.

Gordon Johnstone Remembers

Gordon Johnstone remembers
as a boy how his grannie
gave him half a crown
to clean the box toilet
and spread it on the flower bed:
she had the best
chrysanthemums in town.

He remembers how one day
he found her sitting in the shed
with a tramp playing cards.
He remembers how her house
was the gateway to the Scaur,
that landscape so dear
to his heart.

He remembers how she had
nine children,
two dead young,
and her husband at 39.
He remembers
that she was only five foot tall
but indomitable.

He remembers how
he had a trial
for Auchinleck Talbot,
and went up to her room,
where she said grannie's
lying in for a wee change
but get stuck intae

they Cumnock bastards.
He remembers how,
he came back
to tell her he'd scored
two goals,
got stuck in just as she said,
but she was dead.

Red Letter Day

On the bus back from the clinic,
his face in the racing pages
of the *Daily Record*
Bob grips an envelope.

He says all he has is leftovers,
a few stumps, and the pain isn't them,
those old ghosts of teeth,
but the cancer back again.

I'll no tell the wife.
He rubs his chin:
I'll no tell the wife.
his finger skims the columns,

the disasters and dreams,
the ink that streams
endlessly to the bottom
of the final page.

I'm gan tae walk the dug
and hae some drink,
what else tae dae?
Ma horse might come in:

wud be a red letter day.

Spiral

Sheila, her eyes half closed,
is saying matter of factly
How her life is drawing to an end
and how it's the end of a story,
A spiral some might say:
her father an abuser,
her mother a suicide,
her brother dead young
but it's maybe the morphine
but isn't a spiral a beautiful shape
Like a magical twisting path
like a drill, like a fountain,
like the water that cascades
over the perfect garden
she's kept over the years,
a film of colour that
for a minute feathers the air.

Lost Boy

Fog again today.
The old bridge is deserted,
its hump of spine
curved between lights
that drift like drowned
flower heads.
The breath freezes.
Black water butts stone
and the trees
that fringe the scene
each end, like fingerprints.
There's no point searching:
it has gone, yesterday's river,
with its cold debris,
rushed through the town,
the circle of streets
and doors squeezed
shut like eyes,
gone forever
between dim masonry
and the place you think
the sky should be.

Bells

Bells toll through mist
over wet hills,
nudging towards church,
bed, death.

Terry, ex-soldier,
ex-lamp fitter, ex-coalman,
takes a half while the bells sound,
the spire of St Michael's

shuddering like the mast
of a foundering ship.
He will wet thin lips
and completely disappear

before the final peal,
sunk with the weight
of history,
the lack of present.

Fishy

Who'd have thought all these auld men
were in the SAS. One's asleep
on the bag that once held Bin Laden's head,
but the other two have their beards
primed for a strike in enemy territory,
Moniaive, maybe, if the buses run.
Black Ops they whisper mysteriously.
Black Ops my arse, says the barman,
no more drink for you three nutters.

Tomorrow is another day.
It will roll into place as planned,
it will spill across the zones slowly
like fog, its path tracked precisely,
but now all the liars of the world
are walking home, dreams on their lips.
They will lie below the bright grid of stars,
count drones swimming like fish
in the dark.

Coming out for Caleb

My daughter found Caleb in the park:
the evening was coming on,
it was the beginnings of a cold night.
He was lying in the grass,
waiting for a bumble bee he said,

was allowed out till morning,
no-one would mind.
She took his hand and walked him home
through the last light,
and not only did a bumble bee come,

but a black cat, an old dog,
and even, in the scrub before the scheme,
an anxious hedgehog.
They've all come out for me
cried Caleb.

When she came out at last,
his granny had a wolf tattooed
on each arm.

The Magic Hours

Rain is slippering the paving stones,
the sky a kind of stubble mix
of black and badger grey.
The school kids have tripped home

down the hills from the High St
and the road is ghost empty,
not a single figure,
only some shop fronts lit,

their doors locked hours ago,
though baskets move
in a wind that's gathering,
sending chip papers in the air.

Elsewhere, this time might be spent
drinking coffee by a canal,
opening wine before dinner
as the sun plunges into the sea.

Not here. Day turns to night
with no effective change in tone,
two glum figures swapping shifts
in a job too sad to explain.

In the Hole in the Wall,
Wattie is standing at the bar.
Two weeks ago his son hung himself,
and he has cancer.

In this windowless pub, this salon
of the magic hours, he sings alone.
'To the harbour of my heart
I will send my heart to guide you.'

In Capri or Amsterdam, Honolulu or Siam,
in places like this, no bells,
or assignations, just anxious drinking.
All these hours! Marking time.

The Psychic Detective Jim Gilpin

The Psychic Detective Jim Gilpin
knew that on the Greensands
vampires used to drop from trees
on the backs of passers-by
steal their chips, suck their essence,

dictated three chapters
of the great Dumfries vampire novel
on some weird machine that
engraved symbols on plates
and is still printing,

knew the truth about Elspeth Buchan and Burns
because he had been in the closet
and saw the rapture enfold
like a chimney collapse

in scraped knees and disappointment,
knew for a fact Burns
was slain by Maxwell
because he wandered
between the words and the page

that gap he would haunt particularly
an avenue endlessly
meandering somewhere
between his life and the meaning of it.

The Archive

I think that death
is like corridors
you half remember from school,
the sun diffused
on paint and panel
like a dream.
Here you watched a pretty girl
by a cherry tree,
here you stumbled down a stair,
here are doors closing now like eyes,
pass them by.
Down around this corner
is the last tender archive of the mind
where on this hot afternoon
you must turn off the lights.

Section Two

Hyperborea

Asini/ Callanish

The moon is a shell
set in scrub and rock
a crystal between crags
a blade on the fields

In Hyperborea the moon
balances on the ocean
like a disc while
the stones gleam

Scotland a home of Apollo
Easy to understand
when you see the moon's
tracks on water

like the wake of longships
or Achaean galleys
weaving a net on the world
island by island

linking seas and sea-peoples
before the tyranny
of history books lovingly
tracing coasts like lips.

Grave Goods

I am Adelina beloved of little Damaris:
a fine ginger cat as you can see
from my photogenic flanks
and terracotta whiskers;

no common mouser.
My sisters were blessed by Artemis,
roamed the axis of earth and moon,
turning tides at their whim.

Admire me in my bright lit case.
Tell all I was loyal:
I spent two thousand years in the dark
at that cold child's side.

Parga

In Parga, between Toyota trucks
and the buzz of scooters,
but I have a fine teak table
and a metal jug of wine
beaten like bronze,
and do the brake lights
not gleam like blood on Boetian shields?
This may be Georgio's Greasy Cafe
but behind me are Epirot windows,
loopholes to the sea,
each with its black cowled grandmother,
her last tooth ablaze in the dying sun.

Littoral

The sea is like breathing,
we are drawn to it
with its talk which strangely
is not repetitive
but punctuated by a flow of anecdotes,
ripple and splash,
hilarious sometimes,
fearful at others.

It is an excellent teatime
guest or in the morning
politely waiting for us
just outside
till breakfast is over.
The sea has our story by heart
it will take you to your love,
it will sing while we sleep.

The sea confusingly
is the land's heart,
slowly rubbing away
our attempts at hegemony
indulging us
as any adult would
in our attempts
to swim against the tide.

On the Caul

On the caul,
cormorants balance,
stretch bat wings:
the sun looks through to bone.
Sweat shines on the woman
with the disposable bbq,
she can't believe it,
the bald head of the man
who's doubting there's been
a day like this since 1952,

the bus driver who's gaily
unloosening his tie.
The heat is diamond
and is water too, turning the river
and it's seamless captured sky
into dense reflections,
the town we were or might have been,
kept deep below
and reeded like Atlantis.
It's as if this day has been chosen

above all others
to show that
at the start and end of it,
light crowns us all,
makes us

like mad May Queens,
the way we will be,
the way we were,
when we were small:
bare footed, hot, believing.

Epistle to Robert Burns during a depression in the North Atlantic

Gales fresh across the Atlantic,
the wheelie bins are rattling
the doors like drunkards,
the seas are rising, the rivers, too,
they have come back to
chase the mealie mouthed
back to the bayous
they crawled from.
All these years after
you found light
in a glass of whisky,
a barmaid's eye,
the indomitable soul,
I am sad to announce
the human experiment
has failed in mid Nithsdale.
Hope, health, even colour
have taken the 202 bus
to wherever the fuck it goes,
some hidden deep water cove
where like the fairies
they will sail off somewhere
bright and still alive
to eat small fish
and under a blue sky
think of love and freedom.

Paddy Kelly and the Banjo Tree

Paddy Kelly, sent oan an eerant
by his auld Mither,
wastit a the cash oan lager
an when he wis plaistert
stummled oan a banjo,
takt it hame, gey prood o himsel.
His ma leathered him.
Whit de ye think yer dain
saunterin back here bluitert wi a banjo
ye saucie gowk, an a the siller gan?
Couped it richt oot the windae.
Next day whit do ye think
but a big braw magic banjo tree?
Paddie'd tak a new yin every day
and strum a the way tae the village:
he didnae hae tae be fu tae play it,
but awbody else had tae be
tae thole listenin,
so the hale toon's economy was sauft.

Queran's Well

It's sunk like a navel,
and the stones form a saucer
from an earlier path the experts say,
ripped from an enclosure
that predates everything here.

There have been digs,
and recently they scooped
up coins, some yesterday's,
some old and wafer thin
from the movement in the spring.

The etymology says St Kieran,
the brain says *yesterday*?
There are rags twisted on branches
like gut, for a child sickening,
a love, a journey,

and sun spins through the wish trees,
but they are scrub
no older than me, half formed,
drizzle running down white bark
towards moss and mud.

History is a book, words
crowding to the edge
till there's no room left.
But memories? They are unending
walks in the rain.

Bus station in the wind

The river wild,
blades in the ragged moon.
At shelters
we stand in the stinging breeze,
with pizza crusts or chips,
our apparel nondescript.
It is like our own song sheet,
booth, coffin,
the billowing perspex
we wrap round ourselves,
staring into the night
searching for the holy buses.

Watcher

(In his log, D.A. Mowat, keeper
at Killantringan Lighthouse, Wigtownshire,
records counting 293 moths near his lamp
on the night of 19th September 1913.)

I imagine sailors
watching the lamp's eye,
envious as they creep
along the breast of the sea

like shadows.
From this high place
they are a plank's width
from death,

all questions
drowned on their lips.
I know:
I've seen it.

I am beyond marrying,
watch moths instead of time,
beating on the glass. At night
I sit in the watchroom,

throw my beam of light
like a rope
across the back of the ocean,
and reel in hope after hope after hope.

Crarie Knowe

Harebell and cowslip
are stars in grass,
the hills lit in white
like Himalayan ghosts.
The sun uncoils on long fields,
on trees wound slowly
down the glen to where the river
keeps deep pools.

This is the planet of Mosul
and Aleppo but today it is also
the planet of Crarie Knowe
standing in for the afternoon
the world looks for: a silence,
the people we miss,
the never-ending
dreamwalking home.

Et in Arcadia Ego

A halo of light,
Sudden flame on shop fronts,
on slate, on slick cobblestones
fractured in dazzle:

a glimpse of another place,
a time, a gift from the gods.
This morning in the entrails
of a wet sheep I saw it,

the breath of the Levant,
the fragrance of the Orient,
sometime between half seven
and a quarter to eight,

just before tea,
swelling from the doorway
of Littlewoods,
kindling sandstone,

turning granite
to pearl, copies
of the *Daily Record*
to lost exotic birds.

Come out you
emaciated citizens,
you drunkards and nymphs!
Cast off your oilskins!

When the WiFi's Down

See the darkness belly
behind the streetlight.
Tell the children what fun it is
when the weathers wild.
Don't say you're listening
to that tolling,
too faint and far away
to be the church bell.
Have a drink.
Watch leaves lash on glass
but don't strain to hear beyond
the hollow trees
and the wind on the water.
Put the kids to bed.
Watch the clock crawl,
hope the bell that's ringing
for the dead
across the canopy of time
is a hippy wind chime,
or a small red bucket hammering
against a byre.

Drowned
(to Andrew Greig)

In small towns chip papers
and rags of cloud
move on drowned streets
towards the sea.
When we lift our arms
we are borne away
past broken shop fronts
and half lit pubs,
down cobbles slick
as whaleback.
So much has washed away
from here,
what hangs on is something
not easily defined:
a muddiness one might scorn,
a warmth? That's not it.
A habit.
A way of following your feet,
as they slide,
seeing sky in a pavement.

The Conversion of Sheep

When St Fillian first came upon the sheep
they stood with their Sumerian heads
and stared him out,
for it is a fact that though sheep are mentioned
many times in the bible,
it is always in a bad way.
Follow me said St Fillian,
I have a new path and he pointed
into the hills, to where the sun was rising
setting the gorse to blaze.
They had seen many
paths and sunrises,
you might say they were
inured to them.
They had grass here,
green enough,
and every second Thursday
a book group,
due to discuss that night the third of
Naguib Mahfouz's *Cairo Trilogy*,
illustrating existentialism
in a non-Western context.
Nevertheless they saw
the fine pitch of madness
in the old man's eyes
and, reminding themselves
they were essentially
compliant herd animals,
followed.

Let's Hear it for Homo Naledi

It now transpires that while others
were grabbing the headlines,
the Homo Naledi were chilling
in the soft sediment of a cave nearby,

perpetually unsure whether to walk
or hang from trees,
torn between reverentially stacking
their ancestors' bones

and whacking each other
on the arse with them for a laugh,
never feeling the need
to rise before midday

when they would assemble
on their doorsteps
to chew asparagus
and laugh at the antics

of the Neanderthals next door
whose hairless feet
were already beating
a joyless path to the future.

Nihilists

Dmitry Karakozov's manifesto,
to kill the tyrant Alexander Romanov
and die for his beloved people,
was lost somehow in the post.

Five kopeks were found in his pocket
so perhaps he had forgotten the stamp,
more likely the letter went where
many things go, that unexplained ether

that gathers between good intentions
and hopeless desire.
Maybe it is still in circulation and will land –
plop! – on the door mat of some tall chimneyed
building in St Petersburg when the world is free.

Having shot and missed, Dmitry was asked
by the Tsar what he wanted.
'Nothing much' he is said to have replied,
'Nothing very much at all.'

The Shades of One Shade

When I got up this morning
I saw the glint of a sea loch
in the cup's meniscus,
in the mirror behind my big head,
on the dank hillside like a mirage,
the sheep moving like buoys.
It's the stab of autumn.
Now sick summer's gone
with its smoke and mirrors
we can come into our own:
all the shades of one shade;
our stones, our seas,
our mountain tops,
our cold coming home.

The Lemon Enclosure

I sit every day here
and watch the trees
shift slightly in a breeze
I imagine, never feel.

There are broken strings of birdsong
and traffic on the tarmac shore
is far off like waves.
We are silent mostly:

we come from snow
and the heat thrills us,
beats us flat in sparks like iron.
Though the townsfolk

are wearing parkas,
in the lemon enclosure
there is only light
and rest and waiting.

In the afternoon a child will cry –
a wild baying –
and its mother will
make a gurgled clicking noise

deep in her throat
like a frog or cricket.
We will all listen to this,
with fierce astonishment

and a kind of love,
my daughter, the trees,
the fruit, the wicker fence,
the sparrows.

It is like church should be:
no roofs, no Gods
but sun, and then from quiet corners,
the sacred voices of our own.

Section Three

Ekphrasis

Bacchus and Ariadne
(After the painting by Titian)

See Theseus is away then,
wis it the old
couldnae help it a Goddess telt me to routine?
Load o bull.
Better aff wi me,
weel kent roon here,
pimped ma own chariot,
bit showy but ken how tae party.
Dinnae be pit aff by wee Airchie,
goats' feet run in the family,
wee pun there.
Did you see my Uncle Davy
daein his snake dancing in the X-Factor?
Simon Cowell owes me, hen.
Stick wi me, see your name in lights,
make ye a star.

Circe Poisons the Stream of the Nymph Scylla with Crème de Menthe
(After the painting by John William Waterhouse)

Some places ahve been
they think this IS a love potion.
Let's see if Glaucus' hinging ee
survives yer tongue turnin green
an you oot in the road, sweerin
and threatenin to fight the polis.
Consider yersel honoured:
ahve no skimped wi this,
it's the best o kit.
Only took a crate o Carlsberg
to turn Ulysses' men intae pigs.

Diana and Actaeon
(after the painting by Titian)

Whoa help, sorry wait a meenit there,
whit can I say
last thing ye expect in a wid
six lassies in the scud,
never mind hooseful o women at hame
used tae it, awfie scraps fur the hairdryer,
nice spot fur the alfresco noo the rain's gone hen,
cute wee chihuahua you've got there,
don't suppose you've seen ma dugs
looking fur them,
archery is it, yon's a sport,
Chinese were guid in the Olympics
but you look tasty,
didnae mean that the way it sounded,
what dye mean I've got the horn?
there's ma dugs noo.

Hylas is surprised by Seven Nymphs in a Lily Pond
(after the painting by John William Waterhouse)

Hylas, let us relieve you of that gourd.
No one comes to the spring of Dryope
but we watch them, and you are the fittest yet,
so fit you qualify for our buy one nymph
get six free scheme.
This is a radox bath with added value.
Look at us, Hylas, we're pert
and smooth as grapes,
we don't have stubble like that old Heracles,
with his wine breath and boasting.
Have you asked yourself about these labours,
why he does that kind of stuff?
Over compensation, Hylas.
And don't some folk say he's your Dad?
Even for ancient Greeks, that's sick.
Come on in here past the blossom,
up to your olive thighs then deeper
still. Hylas, look at our lips our eyes,
we'll take you to our green hearts
and you'll never feel dirty again.

Helen of Troy
(after the painting of Jacques-Louis David)

You may lean there, insouciant,
wi your apple cheeks,
It's me that's in the scud,
or was till you draped
that red pepper on my genitals,
that an aphrodisiac in Sparta?
I'm just a boy with a lyre
and a base pedal and a gothic bed
with a goddess strangling a snake, cool eh?
Like a poster for Metallica.
Such a dream having you here,
can't imagine what it'll be like
when you finally undress,
the walls will come down.

Persephone Descends Robustly to the Underworld by Chariot
(after the painting by Carlo Francesco Nuvolon)

Don't despair sisters,
this is the bit I like the best,
the hot breath and hooves,
my chiton streaming in the breeze.

We've hung about half-naked
in the woods all these weeks
and believe me, the sap has risen.
He has his hand on my round belly

but the season for cakes is over.
Look, snow on Mount Helicon:
I go to my bed of coals
and there won't be much sleeping done.

Poetry Doubles, Lesbos
(after the painting *Sappho and Alcaeus*
by Lawrence Alma-Tadema)

Alcaeus

Did you know Jimmy Hendrix pished on this lyre?
We're in the annex of the Aesculapius Memorial Theatre
as Ovid's got a big crowd next door.
Just some eco-poets from Santorini in here,
and my pal Alcetes at the back, drunk again.
Who'll win the famous laurel wreath? Not me.
In Aphrodite's Isle, the girls always win.

Sappho

I'm hurling love's bolt smoking like the sea
but he'd sooner kiss a glass than me,
drink's part of his religion.
So's love, I say, but he's either steaming
or singing dirty songs about boats,
talking of which, I note, the last ferry's gone.
In Aphrodite's Isle, the girls always win.

Section Four

Latro

Lest We Forget

At this time of year let us not forget
to purchase our poppy puppy
bowl and feeding mat
to remember the many poodles who were sacrificed in war,
and the poppy jigsaw
for men in pieces

and the poppy golf balls
for those blown up on the first fairway of the Somme
and the poppy reed diffusers
for soldiers who smelled of fear and shit
and the poppy eco cup holders
for those who returned as vegetables

and the big plastic poppies
for the buses lost in action
at bottlenecks like Verdun.
Now is the time to break
out the poppy picnic basket
for the inconvenient truths
are buried at last with the men
who carried them

and our shock troops now
are menopausal submariners
heavy with badges
and children in fatigues

who will shake their cans
and turn big eyes on you
like Kitchener's,
solemn and dazzling with ignorance.

364 BC

Let us remember the fallen
of the 3rd Sacred War:
these hundred thousand men
with their set jaws,

the blazing sun
on their breastplates.
They died to make the Phocians
keep their cows off temple land.

Their blood will never congeal.
In autumn we will put on
the wild crocus, each petal
hot from a Greek vein.

Let us remember
in the millennia of peace
to come, their rare
and selfless sacrifice.

Jubilation

The British Olympic team
are flying in their gold nosed plane
over the Atlantic. Night has fallen,
stars balance on their wing tips,
lie printed below,
brilliant on the cold grey sea.

It is said they are spending the flight
singing God Save the Queen.
May the ghost of Walter Raleigh salute them,
these brave bicyclists,
may the ghosts of slavers and privateers
who sailed these waters

under that great flag salute them,
the taikwondoers, the golfers,
the rhythmic dancers,
may the ghost of Bobby Charlton salute them,
and he's not even dead.
When I think of the brave sacrifice

of our 5,000 metre runners
on that foreign shore it makes me cry.
They ran so we can be free,
so we can enjoy the television.
I think it was JK Rowling who said
never in a field have so many medals

been won by so few.
And did you notice how
in the papers there were less
car bombings, less immigrants
washed up on beaches?
It was good news for everyone.

Dania Ersheid, on her way home from school

I imagine my beautiful 15-year-old
her head filled with fantasy novels, irony,
her face pasted on the blue screen of the future,
standing at a checkpoint
while soldiers root through her bag
and empty the contents,
school books, tampons,
a pencil case, a key ring,
some small tubes of make-up from Superdrug,
on the ground.

She raises her arms and says
I have no knife
in a confused, surprised tone,
annoyed too because
she doesn't suffer fools gladly,
and then she is shot eight times
and left face down in the dust
 to bleed to death while her killers
shoulder arms and jabber
on their mobile phones.

It is easy to imagine
and likewise impossible.
Injustice rolls on like some juggernaut
too loud and lurid to challenge.
As I read and write this,
my lager on the table,
an autumn night settling outside,
the staff of the pub
are sticking skeletons on glass,
preparing for Halloween.

Overheard in the Buccleuch and Queensberry Hotel

Went fishing with young Dargo,
know him? Black Watch,
worked for FO in Kosovo,
very charming Filipino wife,
no looker but good family,
anyway on Tweed,
beaucoup de booze,
watched the Seven Samurai
then went out with Dick,
Director of BA, wife Sandra,
sensible girl. Fucked up two
Spey Casts in there then caught
a fifteen pound salmon, would
you effin? Had my John Buchan
cloak on, that's why.
You read *Riddle of the Sands*
by Erskine Childers?
First spy novel, shot by
De Valera's mob.
Fancy a trip while the union survives?
Could go to Denmark,
Frisian Islands, some good men there.
All we need is some fucking
Gunga Din to take the luggage.
You ever been on a bus?

Green

The trees are in the water,
knots of bleached roots
and branches,
and green is everywhere,
swollen from deep to lie
on the the loch, on the hills,
on the land that fans away
in the wind forever.
Green has clawed back
masoned stone, pile over pile,
covered our scratch marks,
the monuments to the dead,
the dreams of the living,
all is the same to green:
the colour of sap,
the banner at the foot of the bed.

Today in the Festival,
we will bake our bread,
use our portaloos,
and see the landscape
in songlines,
crafted space and therapy:
tonight we will dance like crabs,
and make shrill noises
through our teeth;
it is our way of showing we are one
with the land, though it sloughs us off
as if we were nothing.

When light comes up once more
like a thin blade we will strike our tepees,
write some applications:
in the studio, make a film called Green.

The Salon, Buccleuch Hotel

Here are some artists.
They are thin and hands
move in their hair
as though the ability to talk
endlessly is dependent on it.
One is working on facial scars:
it is confrontational art, he says.
He has visited Glasgow
but the skin beneath the stubble
is unblemished and, framed in light
through tall windows,
he is like a Madonna,
not the sort that weeps blood.
They are happy to be forming
the narrative, their heads waggle
well into the twilight where outside
the day is dying.
I have sat here for many pints
waiting for the bases to be covered,
for the assurance I need
that the next step on the journey
will not be cursed, betrayed
or end in disaster,
and that if we keep them open wide enough
the sun will always pour from our mouths.

Peace in Our Time

'I Left my Fish Cakes in the World's End'
would be a great title for a poem,
like 'Sheep are Hard Bastards',
or 'That's what Happens to Porridge Sometimes'.
How much better than 'Adlestrop'
or 'She Walks in Beauty like the Night',
which make no sense at all.
When I think of the titles of all the unwritten poems,
tripping innocently from tongues
under endless sun or stars, it makes me weep.
Look, we must, right now – Now! –
drop our spades and screens,
our cake forks and rifles,
and write the poems our titles need.

Markers

A land of markers, Galloway,
even the fancy cathedrals
turned to rubble, shells
for the rain to seep through.

We carry our histories deep.
In ports long gone
slabs of ballast sit,
still licked by an exhausted sea.

Persian limestone,
Otago basalt,
granite from Chile,
and near these cairns

washed here
on the currents of the world,
jewels to outblink the sun.
Pressed in Galloway glaur,

but bright as stars,
and like real stars, frozen
at the moment of extinction,
shining still across the years

to show here once was a *land*,
and *here,* its history, its story hoards.

Silk with a White Eagle

Silk with a white eagle
they say was how the Turks
recognised the corpse of the King
ridden down at the gate.

The idea of the Emperor's last stand
had thrilled me since
Bill Smith at school painted
the scene with words like knives.

Byzantium and Byzantine silk,
so far removed
from the muddy foothills
of Dumfries and its monuments

like little teeth. It was the end
of the world he said.
A bit like Dumfries on
a Sunday night in October,

only flames, bombard,
the cries of the damned.
When I heard Byzantine silk
had turned up here

It was like saying someone
had uncovered a pot of dreams,
the meeting of impossible worlds
made possible by men

who lived here long before
us, before the Emperor
himself was tombed in legend.
It made me cry for my mad old teacher,

his passion, his life
uncommemorated.
It gives me hope good stories
will always surface, stay good.

Reflections on Heritage in a Galloway Harbour

Poleaxed sprawled side on in the mud
like some brassed off weekender
left when the bus drove off,
stranded by lifeless water
and the sodden flanks of hills.
Galloway – see it if you're lost
or a hippy or wonder
where Martin Bell ended up –
or if you're a star gazer,
no firelight there
just the rose petal light
of online *Daily Mail*s
in the slippered dusk.
The call of the curlew,
the call of the wind turbine,
the call of the metal detector,
the vote no boards propped up
in barns like old archery butts,
ready for the next time,
 the time after that,
the time after that.
Low energy currents,
on a landscape that's slipped off life
like a skin and left ribs of stone.
I stand in the dry mouth
of the harbour
and my throat is parched too.
Out there once in the mist
the arteries of nations

currachs, knars, galleys,
Alan Lord of Galloway
sneering at King John for
crapping it at Runnymede,
but history left
with the ships
to Pictou and Prince Edward Island,
the trains to Birmingham.
Where are the harpists
and the tale tellers now?
The tinkers, the fairies,
the road builders?
No camps,
no publight even to shine in.
Coaches ply between ghost towns
with ghost cargoes.
Night is funnelling down the channels,
only sounds to conjure with now,
the faraway throb of a jukebox
a newspaper gutted by the wind,
a car, cleaving through puddles.
Save the Viking Hoard:
for who?

Mongrels

With Robert Burns a sex pest,
Irn Bru diluted to prevent
seizures
and Greyfriars Bobby
exposed as a clever gang
of street dogs,
we must doubt even more
the props of our race

and ask whether vowels
and a confused grasp
of history
are the only things separating
we noisy people from
the wee noisy people down there.
Last night while spruces shook
beyond the window

I watched a woman singing
Biodh an Deoch:
her voice was like the
sea you hear when young,
broken and beautiful with
yet to be defined sorrow.
Chunnacas bat' air an fhairge.

She could have been singing
from a dessert menu
and I curse the folk who
barred me from my mother's tongue,
mealy mouthed red faced
pointless folk,
like me.

Rummaging in a Box on St Andrews Day

Sometime in the black and white era,
a man clips a sheep by a dyke.
Behind him a thin strip of land
tapers to tall trees.
The sheep on the tressle table
shakes a thin flapper's leg
at sullen skies.
The dyke could be any dyke,
the thin strip of land any thin strip of land,

only he knows what is behind the camera,
where the road took his boots
that evening,
which huddle of houses,
which hearth, which bairns,
which bible.
He is smiling under a rakish cap.
I imagine he came home from the war,
likes a dram. Salt of the earth.

Scotland is guessing like this:
how we pack the space between what we believe
and what we don't want to.
We use old books,
old songs, old solidarities,
memories of the relatives we knew,
exclude wife beaters and psychopaths,
gossips and closet sadists,

and from the remaining handful
we weave a story fit for
land and seascapes
so beautiful they hurt.
Tonight if my sore leg permits,
and the moon is full,
I will walk down the glen
to where my people are waiting.
They will turn their faces
to me and we will imagine
past times to come.

Scotland's Hidden Gems

In the hotel here there's a painting
of Eilean Donan Castle,
as if that merciless piece of touristry
had been transported to the Rain Forest.
Huge spoons of leaves loll round the eyes
as they peer through lush and savage trees.
Though by an amateur it is a work of genius,
and how I long to see her other work:
the Scott Monument in the Marianas Trench,
furred by barnacles and occasionally
illuminated by electric fish;
Balmoral on the surface of the sun;
the Duke of Sutherland's statue
inverted down some giant toilet bowl.
I'm not the artist, but I'd call the series
Scotland's Hidden Gems.

September 2014

On top of Dunreggan,
the sky is white and burns like a crown.
Far off, a helicopter
hangs over a wood,
its gruffness the only sound
apart from wind,
which is not a sound but a freshness,
a kind of freedom on the skin.
There's poetry here
the land is clodded with it,
the great hills images to be broken up,
the grass streaming like words.
I am the only person here,
this heady day,
and I am balancing the sun
on one finger,
holding everything at bay
for a dream.

Section 5

Oikia

Birthday

It'd been a long day,
the wind howling down the road,
the bulbs failing.
I was thinking in a way

what a trail and what's the end
when you're this age and
your weans polite but detached
and dreams somewhere

stashed in a drawer,
then in the kitchen suddenly
the oldest one
said do you know

the Canadian Barn Dance?
I swear the longest sentence
I'd had over a month
was eight words

but she went on: start
with that foot, walk
for three steps, hop,
walk back for three and hop,

move sideways, clap,
waltz, sideways again,
to the left then back,
dance round the room,

dance round the room!
What a speech,
and how her braces shone
in the failing light!

There was four foot square
to move in, only a space
between table
and piles of plates

but we danced and danced.

A Proper Joke

Through a haze of noise,
late night juke box anthems
and the beginnings of a fight,
the door bangs open,
and a blast of cold air heralds
the entry of my Uncle Jack.
He is dressed in a short sleeved
shirt and flannel trousers,
with a comical moustache
like an ink line perched above
his mouth.

It is odd to see him
like this, exactly like I
remember him,
odder still
as he is dead.

He stands at the bar,
and the air between us is filled
with a slight turbulence,
as though sentences should be there.
I cannot remember a single word
from my Uncle Jack

though it was known
he was a funny man,
holding people's head under
the water until their ears
felt like bursting.
He and my father were close

because of the war:
it is said they both went bald
on the same day.
The last time I saw them,
in Edinburgh in 1973,

they didn't know who I was,
and I never said.
I didn't like Uncle Jack.
What he's doing here now,
when I myself am losing hair,
and so much complex time
has passed, and he is surely dust
long lost by the shores
of the North Sea, is a mystery.
Perhaps it is his idea, at last,
of a proper joke.

Psalm 121

I remember her saying,
I lift my eyes to the hills.
Summonses would arrive,
cheques bounce knee high,
stones fall from the roof,
she would lift her eyes to the hills.
Through desertions and disasters,
her eyes to the hills.
Through disease at the end, the hills.
I thought her faith misplaced
but now I see it was not for
the consolation of The Lord
she lifted her eyes to the hills,
but the memory of another time and place:
bright rain lifting on the brae road,
a dog running through the broom,
her mother waiting at the door.

Castle Building

Two sets of bastioned walls,
each section notched
and interlocked.
In the barbicans bridges

pulled by string
portcullises the same.
A keep pinnacled with corbels
and below, talus scrim.

No ladder could stand
against that slope.
For anyone who stumbled
past the arrow slits

there were tiny murder holes.
It was impregnable, sealed,
and each piece of plywood
and pennant painted

to mimic brick or silk.
Legend says the builder
left us without a word
no kiss, no sign, no letter,

just a fortress no soldier
would ever take. I see
his bent back
the scarred fingers,

the brush and blade.
His war would have no end.
Like the knights he hid
his voice in stone,

in abandoned parapets.
For years the castle stood,
through childhood, a cypher,
I see now, for regret and care

and guilt, inked and cut
through winter months
of painstaking work:
love in other words.

Last Post

My father said they played
the last post for him,
but he was confused I think.
It's true he was in the morgue
when he twitched his way
back to his life: our lives;

back from the brink
of god knows. My father
was a spiritualist, believed
the dead lived again.
When he talked of his pain
and guilt as the aircraft

corkscrewed down
he was talking to them,
the ones who never made it.
Did he indulge them
too much, these ones?
Did they go on to hang

on his every living word,
nudge his arm,
fur his tongue,
fill his black wells
of eyes
with their burning oil?

Late

Every morning I passed a plaque
on my way to school.

I was usually hurrying, late,
but the plaque was to the late

Norman Anderson
so it caught my fancy.

In the ten minutes
winding down the wee road

beside the river I was always
wondering why Norman Anderson

was late and what he was late for:
something important obviously,

some battle, some meeting,
something that disappointed folk

when he didn't show.
I wondered also if he ever

tried getting to bed earlier
or setting the alarm at another time,

or whether he was like me
just doomed to be late,

walking up these grey steps
every morning to a door already shut.

Bryony Paterson and the Poetry Machine

I am charging a pound:
Xmas verses for fat hubbies,
friends with cats,
old ladies who love gardening.

A pun, a rhyme, some schmaltz,
the whole thing not making art,
but maybe by tea time,
if I'm lucky, three pints.

Then a girl arrives.
I explain how the machine works:
the form is put in the box,
goes up the live line to cloud

where the magic is –
in reality me scribbling in another room.
After a while she returns.
This is for Thomas, she's written,

his voice is a wonder,
his smile lights up my world,
and I hope if he gets this poem,
he might be my first love?

She waits, is waiting still,
for nothing will get better than this:
the drab afternoon is blazing
and the poem she needs

is already written.

My Birthday

The day I was born
I always say, the clouds were black,
it was cold for March,
and my father's mother
was adding some upper Nithsdale
aggro to an already tricky situation:

a typical west highland inspired home birth,
the sheets billowing like sails,
a stiff breeze, a stiff malt,
a boy born in angst and squall.
All that is written in stone,

but now, at this late date, you tell me
that all that morning you searched
for a gift of crocuses,
found eight purple, one white,
and bore them up the stairs with love,

and now I must revise my history forever
to include the blessing of the little girl below,
picking crocuses.

Janice

Skirting the strip of waste
and rubble that was our gardens,
I find a splintered tooth of wood
and I am suddenly holding the hand

of Janice Skupine as she smiles
broadly across the fence her father
has just turned bright red.
There is the smell of fresh paint

and honeysuckle and the noise
of bees buzzing like they did,
drowning thought.
She was six and I was seven

and this place had not seen concrete
and a pear tree was a pavilion
where we all crouched
dreaming of the present.

Janice never stopped smiling
I realise now,
though she was the first to go,
to Australia, in the way

things happened then,
one moment leaning through a fence
and smiling, the next in Australia.
I waited for her to come back

the following day, long after,
and only gave up
when a new family arrived,
with no daughters.

I wonder what the world
wants of us
that it scatters us like smoke
across the grass,

and leaves these things
in our minds,
beautiful and useless,
like broken glass.

Road Trip

When a mechanic announced
my mother's car was dead,
the metal eaten away,

she did not, as we expected,
cancel our road trip,
but cheerfully extended it

to include the time taken every ten miles
to stop and fill the radiator.
We had a pail

in the back seat and more,
every tap and burn and loch
from Moffat to Cape Wrath.

It was unseasonably sunlit
and the land itself unwrapped
before us, like some gift:

waves echoed,
birds soared,
moors glittered at night like coal.

No blazing longship
could have matched that mission.
Steered with eccentric joy

that dying Morris
is my emblem for Scotland yet:
love, and doggedness.

Rosemary is Remembering

Rosemary is for remembering
Ophelia said, before she drowned.
I am rubbing it near my nose
and all the wash of smut
and sweat and irritation is drained
and we are in a garden,
you are spilling herbs
into my top pocket.
It is hot summer,
your hair gleams below
the little cloth band
you bought with
your pocket money.
I see it all. I smell it all.
How can I tell you
about such remembering?
Your smile: that smile.

Reading *Electric Brae* before the Plane

Time passes in intensities of heat.
I'm half reading, half dozing,
in a little courtyard,
in a cloister of a little courtyard,

each paved stone
ten thousand pinpricks of fire,
each scruffy tip of grass kindling,
the square of sky sore blue

with only a faint apostrophe of cloud.
There's beer in my bag
and I am relishing
the chemistry Cruzcampo will add

to this lush precipice of time.
I am half in half out of the story,
will they won't they?
Will I won't I?

Though I read the book every year,
I still don't know.
Like the sun I flit between the characters,
their faults, their loves, light on each one.

The Airwaves

The profile of Scottish hills
make words I would send
in esoteric ways:

sunlight is a wavelength,
so is shadow and birdsong
and the tap of fingers on glass.

Whole vocabularies pass this way,
while the moon blinks on and off,
the world turns,

kids grow leggy like fawns..
Someone's night is always alive
with sentences

rhythmic and sleepless as cicadas,
punctuated now and ever,
with love.

The Nymphaeum

The stream glitters
through the trees like eyes,
all is hush and moving,
the birds, the breeze,
the girls' hair.
I could stay here
I say, in this shade.
See the light on the water?
Hear its voice? They nod.
Jasmine is talking
of the Goddess' skin tone
while Lydia searches for 3G.
We share many times like these,
spinning below the sun and stars,
staring at the same space
and seeing different things.
I could stay here some more,
but to the nymphs themselves,
it's just another door.

Where the Burn joins the River

Where the burn joins the river
the language of water is verbs,
rushing from the hills and the fields
with the wind that breaks

the surface in flakes of glass
that mob and scatter like birds.
My daughter is often there:
for now, it is the boundary

of her empire. She sits for hours.
Sentences form, break apart,
and then move away always
towards the sea.

The Christmas Box

The pine needles
in floorboards
and the seams of scarves
will be reminders
of the time when in spite
of all evidence
we like to dream,

but the rest is packed
in tissue thin as silk:
the gold thread,
the ceramic stars,
the glass cockatoo,
the little frosted birds
in their straw nests.

Every year I wonder
how changed we'll be
when it's unpacked again,
whether the snow will lie,
whether the sheep and I
will be around to chew insouciantly
and count cold stars.

A neighbour left,
one moment cheerily
mislaying his bus pass,
the next wandering,
his brain knotted
like a burst golf ball.
He lies broken in the box,

which I lift with one hand
as it is light, full of fabulous
air and mirrors, keeping
through endless months
the blurred images,
our angles trapped
for a while, in golden glass.

Section Six

Foteinos

Tuesday Night, Ciutadella

Fronds hung with water like rope,
fat and white as opals.
It is good to be off your head
somewhere new, where the rain
has a different slant, fast and loud
and desperate to get to ground.
The sea has no end and talks long
into the night like a mother tongue.
I sit and drink and watch puddles spread
and shimmer, while my girls,
happy in all migrations, sing like birds.

Poetry

I think this is
where poetry is,
shouldering the old man
between the pint and the taxi.
It's between the thought and the action,
the need and the reality.
It's between the street lamp and the sky,
the page and the pencil,
the blood and the skin.
It's that piece of electricity
between the sting and the poison.

Hope

The moon is held in cloud
but the tide of sky will wash it
rare and blue like shell
over the familiar skyline
with its scree, its rime.

Elsewhere I know the sun
is spilling over water and tile,
desert and fat green leaf.
I am guessing all over the planet
we are picked out like this,

by the clock-face of light,
in our glorious windows,
wadis, forests and trains,
silhouetted in moments
of perfect, lucid despair.

Christmas is a time of hope
though it is not delivered
from the night sky
by sleigh or cross or Amazon.
Hope is the last tool in the box.

Hope is Dareen Tatour
in that courtroom arguing
hour after hour
that poetry is truth.
Hope is keeping opening your mouth.

Nativity

Nothing less like Christmas.
Just constant twilight,
though twilight is too nice,
more the sun's on dim,

the rain on repeat,
only through the prism
of decorations swaying
on their plastic hawsers

on walls and shop fronts
do we have light,
pound shop light,
oily circles rubbed

by fingers in the gloom.
But maybe hope
will be born here
in the dirty doorway

of the Spar, or the Tattoo Shop,
by stacks of unsold
Daily Records, and boxes
of cut price Xmas pies.

Wet terriers will
come, their tails will fan
wonderful puddles,
lorries will sing

on their way north,
old men will pause,
and maybe in the strange
collision of these trajectories

folk will search
through clouds and smoke
and debris, and long months
of cruelty, to find a star.

Nunc Scio Quid Sit Amor

There's a swallow next door,
its neck is flame in the setting sun,
its breast white as it presses
for a crack in the window or door
between broken shafts of wood
and empty paint pots.
Outside, its mate
hangs on the ledge,
their heads only a tiny transparency
apart, an illusion of togetherness:
one in sunlight, one in shadow.
Seven thousand miles through
hot angles of air,
through desert, jungle and reed bed,
and now only mirror motions of love.
A small beating on glass.

That Time of Night

Through the window in the half dark
the congregation of trees shake their
palms in prayer and sheep gruffly
discuss another day without drink.
I was dreaming of you, but I'm finished
with poems now and full of gin I crave
the emptiness of glass. The truth is
I'm ready to take my place on the gantry.
Prise the moon from its wall of night!
I want to fill with clouds of light
and throw reflections round the room.
I want to prism, spin and keep on spinning.

Lit

The gulls' lazy laughter,
breaking the oily surface of street
for chip papers.
The coats are off,
nymphs at the fountains
take selfies.
Dumfries is unseasonal:
someone's actually just said
we'll suffer for it. I raise
a golden neck of beer
to Alasdair Reid, Willie Neill,
to the dead poets of Galloway:
the land is laid open for you
like a shining leaf.
To the living ones,
the sun drops words in our palms,
poetry will come today from
sand and scrim,
from alleyway and bar,
from burn mouth and glen,
from the shining eyes
we have, we imagine.
Watch!
We will shake our words over
golden cobblestones.

Luath Press Limited

committed to publishing well written books worth reading

LUATH PRESS takes its name from Robert Burns, whose little collie Luath (*Gael.*, swift or nimble) tripped up Jean Armour at a wedding and gave him the chance to speak to the woman who was to be his wife and the abiding love of his life. Burns called one of the 'Twa Dogs' Luath after Cuchullin's hunting dog in Ossian's *Fingal*. Luath Press was established in 1981 in the heart of Burns country, and is now based a few steps up the road from Burns' first lodgings on Edinburgh's Royal Mile. Luath offers you distinctive writing with a hint of unexpected pleasures.
Most bookshops in the UK, the US, Canada, Australia, New Zealand and parts of Europe, either carry our books in stock or can order them for you. To order direct from us, please send a £sterling cheque, postal order, international money order or your credit card details (number, address of cardholder and expiry date) to us at the address below. Please add post and packing as follows: UK – £1.00 per delivery address; overseas surface mail – £2.50 per delivery address; overseas airmail – £3.50 for the first book to each delivery address, plus £1.00 for each additional book by airmail to the same address. If your order is a gift, we will happily enclose your card or message at no extra charge.

Luath Press Limited
543/2 Castlehill
The Royal Mile
Edinburgh EH1 2ND
Scotland
Telephone: +44 (0)131 225 4326 (24 hours)
Email: sales@luath.co.uk
Website: www.luath.co.uk